Until we meet

again

your thoughts deserve
a decent place
to live

until

we

meet

again

for the little girl who
dreamed of airplanes,
shooting stars,
and happy endings
i hope the woman i have become
would make you proud

Route

A note from me to you

These words were never written to be shared.

They were written as I backpacked through Europe
in the summer of 2019. Scribbled in my journals
day by day, week by week, country by country,
at a time in my life when I was in a constant desperate hope
of discovering something deep within that could magically fix
everything that hurt. Turns out, healing is never linear.
I had to learn that the hard way. Things don't happen
the way we want. People disappoint, take advantage, leave—
but in these pages I am here to show you so much more
than just what went wrong.

I want to show you something real, to show you
persistence, to show you the ups and downs we all know
too well of an aching heart, to show you the
attainable goodness within this world.
The true wonder that exists in the fine details.
In the strangers. In the wildflowers.

I need to show you how I was finally able
to say goodbye.
This entire book, months later,
to me now— is a goodbye. To him. To a part of me.
To what I thought I understood about love.

These pages are here now to show you the magic
that is possible for those who go looking for it.
The magic that is raw human emotion.
Connection. Loss. Empathy. Hope.
Yes, that magic even exists in the bad days,
the lost time, and in every broken piece of your heart.
It lives in every breath.
I was afraid to share these words at first,
afraid it was too real, messy, raw, imperfect— until I realized
that is the very reason it should be shared.

If you have found this book, it's for a reason.
I can only hope that through my story
you might come closer to courage—
to let go of what burdens your heart.

xx - R

New York City

May 7th, 2019
Plane to New York City

The light that is shattered
across the inside of the plane cabin
reminds me of the pieces of my heart
that I've chipped away for those
who never wanted me.
A certain kind of loneliness
is following me like a shadow
and even though I hope with flying
five thousand miles away
I can escape it— I know
it won't go away that easy.

I'm plagued by the wanting.
I have so much love to give
and I don't know what to do with it.

As the plane lands I look over
and my friend is laughing
through the fear in her eyes,
knowing we've made it.
In this moment I smile
and I let the warmth in
for as long as I can
until the cold comes back.

May 8th, 2019
36,000 ft above the Atlantic Ocean

I have been carrying this loss, this doubt,
this regret, this burden of dissatisfaction
for so long that it has become
indistinguishable from gravity itself.
Maybe that's why I can feel, so intensely,
the pull of the moon—
maybe she's trying to take away
some of the heaviness,
but I hold onto it too tight.
I don't know what I would be
without it.

Everyone has always told me
to keep my head out of the clouds.
To be grounded.
Well, this weight in my chest
sure as hell keeps me grounded,
that's for certain.
But what if they're wrong?
What if I was meant to fly?

The plane is taking off now and
soon I will be halfway across the world.
I have to believe I can only take
so much of this heaviness with me—
Some will be left behind.
Some will follow.
But at least in this moment
suspended in time & sky—
I am weightless.

Madrid, Spain

May 9th, 2019
Madrid, Spain

I am finding wonder
in this life once more.
In the cold night air that blows
the curtains wildly around the room,
hearing languages I don't understand,
sharing endearing moments with strangers
that I will never see again.

This place reminds me what it is like
to feel alive in every beating
moment.

Here,
I will learn how to be
present. I will learn
how to be satisfied. I will learn
how to fall madly in love
with every little detail
and I will learn
how to let it all
go.

May 10th, 2019
Parco del Retiro
Madrid, Spain

This is my meditation: alone.

I'm surrounded by a symphony
of unfamiliar bird songs,
innocently wild daisies,
ducklings bobbing in calm water,
sunlight playing in the ripples.

Reflections distorted
but full of color & beauty—
just like my
memories
of this moment will
one day be. I feel at peace here.
I feel a thousand years old
and I feel brand new. I feel
reborn
in the afternoon sun.

Barcelona, Spain

May 11th, 2019
Off the coast of Barcelona, Spain

There are times in my life
when I am a boat tied to a dock. I feel
trapped,
but I also feel safe.
It's easy to spend all my days like this—
never having to fear the uncertainty of
open water or a terrifyingly endless
horizon brimming with the unknown—

but I was crafted
to sail the oceans of the earth
and the days when I am untied,
free, directionless
are the days I beg you
to believe that
we are made
to do so much more
than just
exist.

May 12th, 2019
The shores of Badalona, Spain

The wind blows
strands of hair
across my face and plays
with the folds of my clothing.
To the sound of the waves— I give
everything I am and ask
for nothing in return but a moment
of tranquility.
The shapes behind my closed eyes form
shadows of the laughter
that surrounds me.
When the voices of music
whisper my favorite song
my heart
takes flight with the sea breeze
and learns of all the places it has been.

This soul of mine has always been
a dreamer of sorts
and when I open my eyes—
the moon is there,
high above the horizon,
shining faintly through soft daylight,
watching over me
with a crescent smile.

May 13th, 2019
Barcelona, Spain

I've always believed hearts that break
should go to Europe— in the past,
I admit I was running away
from the pain, but this time
I brought it all with me,
packed carefully
into my backpack, and here—

surrounded by challenges
at every turn
that I have no choice
but to overcome,

I am becoming a believer
that maybe, just maybe
I can finally
overcome
you,
and somehow find
myself
again.

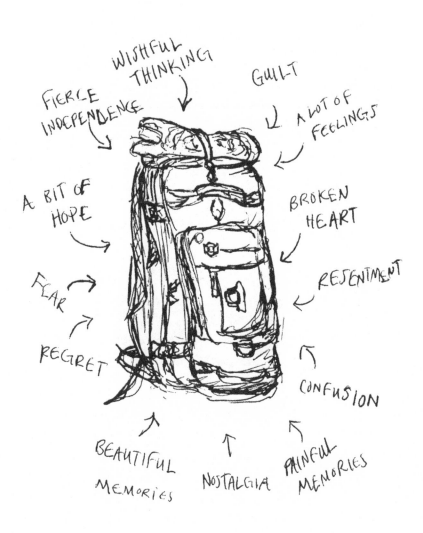

WISHFUL THINKING

GUILT

FIERCE INDEPENDENCE

A LOT OF FEELINGS

A BIT OF HOPE

BROKEN HEART

FEAR

RESENTMENT

REGRET

CONFUSION

BEAUTIFUL MEMORIES

NOSTALGIA

PAINFUL MEMORIES

May 14th, 2019
Somewhere in the Mediterranean Sea

Can you imagine flying
alone
for years over the open ocean without
ever touching solid ground?

I understand the desire for travel,
but I also have roots
to nourish, even when I'm gone.

An albatross bird
has braver wings than I,
and I have to be okay with that.
I have to be okay
with never being as free
as I may want to be.

There is beauty in being
tethered,
and when I close my eyes I can see it
in the smile of my mother
and her arms wide open—
welcoming me back
home.

May 15th, 2019
Venice, Italy

It's getting late and I've written
pages and pages and I can't get this right.
These words feel as empty as my chest
and I don't know what to do.
You're gone, why can't I just accept
that you
are
gone.
You're never coming back.
You don't even want to see me
and I have to pretend that's
okay.
How do I forget you? How do I open
my heart to someone else when I don't
even remember where I hid it? How
do I close my eyes and not remember
your arms wrapped around me or your
calloused hands holding mine?

How do I not feel cold. all. the. time.

Please tell me how to forget
the way you first looked at me
like you had finally found something
you had always been searching for.
How do I forget the day you left?
How do I forget the moment you shattered
my heart when you chose addiction over me?
How do I put this into words in some kind of
elegant way when I feel absolutely & completely
numb to anything that is beautiful.
How do I stop searching for you
in train stations despite knowing
you'll never be there? How do I lay down at
night and not wish for you to be beside me?

Venice, Italy

The world is wide and I feel alone in it now
more than ever.

How do I feel that kind of love again
without you? Am I even meant to feel
that kind of love again?
Sometimes I think I'm not cut out for it—
not anymore. Sometimes I think I was
designed to be alone.
Something about leaving you behind damaged me
beyond repair. Or maybe it was long after,
when I saw you again in her arms,
when I couldn't even recognize
the man you had become. I don't know how to
make this poetic anymore. I'm tired.
I'm broken.
When you left, you took my heart with you
and I want it back—
but
I don't want you to forget me.
Even though, I'm sure you already have.

May 16th, 2019
Venice, Italy

What if I were to float
away
in this gondola—
set adrift amongst
the endless labyrinth
of winding passageways and canals,
lost in a fairytale,
never to be tied down again.

Would I then, finally,
be happy?

Maybe if I just completely lose
myself
in this place, and find
some kind of love
within,
I will be able to forget
what it has ever felt like
to be left
behind.

VENEZIA

ISBN 978-88-7393-029-7
9 788873 930297
I 112
Edizioni D'Arte I.M. Firenze
printed in Italy

May 2019
16th

my angel,
I will never send you these postcards.
I am writing to hope you are well, When will I heal?
and to ask — after all this Will I ever heal?
time — why can't I move Will I ever fall in love
forward? I've gotten to where again? Do I ever want to?
I've accepted we will never
be together and that has to
be the best thing for us both —
but it doesn't heal me.
Why am I still broken? —R

May 16th, 2019 - Venice, Italy

My Angel,

I will never send you these postcards. I am writing to hope you are
well, and to ask — after all this time — why can't I move forward?
I've gotten to where I've accepted we will never be together and that
has to be the best thing for us both — but it doesn't heal me.
Why am I still broken? When will I heal? Will I ever heal?
Will I ever fall in love again?
Do I even want to?

-R

Verona, Italy

May 17th, 2019
Train to Verona, Italy

What did you do to me?
It barely even takes a word
for you to completely derail every
thought I ever had that
I've moved past this.
Do you want to keep me
from being able to breathe
because I can't
when the broken pieces of my heart
are stabbing into my lungs.

One moment I feel like I'm flying
and in the next you come out of
silence and knock me down,
breathless,
helpless,
hopeless—

and by the time I look up
you're already gone.

May 18th, 2019
Juliet's Tomb
Verona, Italy

Dear Juliet,

I've left a little garden flower
on your tomb to bring life
to this empty place.
You were full of so much
courage & grace, yet here I am
defeated—
I can't imagine surrendering
anything for love.
I don't even know how to give
myself
to love.
I only know how to run from it.
I only know how to
regret. But here,
in this place— I can feel
your spirit, your essence
begging me to try.
The cool air feels like it's washing over
my sinking heart, a current pushing
it to the surface, taking away the
fear with a hopeful breath.

This is when I have to trust you, I have
to trust all the broken hearts who have
come here before me searching for
answers, I have to trust myself,
and I have to try. Somehow.
I can almost hear you whisper in the
wind— try, try again.

VERONA

I 128

ISBN 978-88-7393-374-8

printed in Italy

Edizioni D'Arte I.F.I. Firenze

My angel,
I walked through the city today on my own, to find a place where I could breathe. I never found it. I wondered what it would be like if you were walking beside me, but when I looked over— it was always a stranger. I wish I wouldn't imagine you. It would be nice to have your hands to hold. It was cold today & no matter what I did— I could never warm up.

—R

May 2019 18th

May 18th, 2019 — Verona, Italy

My Angel,

I walked through the city today on my own, to find a place where I could breathe. I never found it. I wondered what it would be like if you were walking beside me, but when I looked over— it was always a stranger. I wish I wouldn't imagine you.
It would be nice to have your hands to hold. It was cold today & no matter what I did— I could never warm up.

—R

May 19th, 2019
Verona, Italy

I wandered through the winding streets
of this tired old city today,
and I couldn't shake this sinking feeling.
It was raining, cold and constant,
but I went anyway. I felt like I was
searching for something
that I was never going to
find.
I got to the point where I felt
like I was
suffocating. I don't know what
happened,
but I couldn't stop it
so I just let it
happen.
I still feel like I lost
something.
Something important. I don't think
I'll ever find it.
No matter how
far
I walk. No matter how long
I look. I'll never
find
him.

May 20th, 2019
The Juliet Club
Verona, Italy

I can't help but feel like an imposter,
claiming the name "Juliet" as my own
and promising a kind of love
to all of these
broken young hearts
when I don't even know if it exists.

If this ingenuine ink
that bleeds from my pen,
assuring them that love will come,
is all I can give—
am I only giving them lies?
I wish I could give them more.

I wish I could
save them from heartache—
but how am I supposed to save them
when I can't even
save myself?

Florence, Italy

May 21st, 2019
Galleria dell'Accademia
Florence, Italy

How can I claim to be an artist
while gazing up at a true masterpiece?
The greatest art in history
has already been made—
in marble, in canvas, in novel, in poetry,
so why do we even bother?
Maybe it's not about being
one of the greats— maybe it's about
carving your heart out of your chest,
painting the world in your own way,
sharing stories that matter to you
no matter who is listening,
and stringing words together in the
fragile hope
of simply making
people feel
something.
Maybe art
is what keeps us
alive.

May 21st, 2019 - Florence, Italy

My Angel,

I saw a man today who reminded me of you. As he put a cigarette
between his lips— for a moment I could see your face. Your lips.
You always used to hand roll your cigarettes, though— his were
store bought. I also didn't see his eyes— but I know they wouldn't
be able to look at me like yours. But his lips— he had your lips.
I didn't miss them until today. I wish I didn't miss them—
but I do. I miss their words, I miss looking at them while you talk,
I miss the feeling of them all over me.
But I still wish I didn't miss them at all.

                                                        -R

May 21st 2019

21c. Firenze - La Badia e il Bargello, da Piazza S. Firenze
da un acquarello di Yousuf Obaid

My angel,
I saw a man today who reminded
me of you. As he put a cigarette
between his lips— for a moment
I could see your face. Your lips.
You always used to hand roll your
cigarettes though, his were store bought.
I also didn't see his eyes—
but I know they
wouldn't be able
to look at me like yours.

But his lips—
he had your lips.
I didn't miss them until
today.
I wish I didn't miss them—
but I do.
I miss their words, I miss
looking at them while you
talk, I miss the feeling of
them all over me.
But I still wish I didn't miss
them at all.

ARTS & CRAFTS
Il Palastino
Via Guglielmo Marconi, 3r 50131 Firenze
Tel. e Fax. 055 289918
www.italianwatercolor.com
e-mail: ilpalazzano@virgilio.it

May 22nd, 2019
Manarola, Cinque Terre
Italy

In this place I have known fear
and I have known
what it takes to overcome.
From being the last one to jump,
shaking and afraid—
to leading the recklessness
into the crystal blue depths
to be surrounded
by glistening effervescence
and to surface anew—
courageous.

It's been quite some time
since that first day I chose to
trust myself—
but I can still feel the bravery
coursing through these veins—
forever a part
of the beating of my heart.

May 22nd, 2019 – Manarola, Italy

My Angel,

I don't really know why I'm writing you. You'll never see this and I don't even know if I really miss you. Maybe I'm writing because you're the only man who has ever said "I love you" and made me believe it— even if it was never meant to last. I know it was never meant to— I never even really wanted it to. But for some reason I was still absolutely shattered when you left. Maybe I missed the feeling more than you. I just don't know. I only know I'm terrified to open up to anyone else ever again & I've tried everything & I'm still not healed. I don't know what else to do— so I will keep writing to you until I figure it out.

                                        –R

Riviera Ligure
Le Cinque Terre
Manarola

SANREMO

May 22nd 2019

RV 6686

My angel,
I don't really know why I'm writing you. You'll never see this and I don't even know if I really miss you. Maybe I'm writing because youre the only person who's said "I love you" and made me believe it— even if it didn't last. I know it was never meant to— I never even really wanted it to.

But for some reason I still got absolutely shattered when you left. Maybe I missed the feeling more than you. I just don't know. I only know I'm terrified to open up to anyone else ever again + I've tried everything + I'm still not healed. I dont know what else to do. So I will keep writing to you until I figure it out. –R

Foto: A. Scapin

May 22nd, 2019 — Pisa, Italy

My Angel,

I'm leaving Pisa now— I was only reminded of you once. In a single pair of blue eyes— but his looked at me like a stranger. That's how your eyes would look at me now, I'm sure. You would've either loved Pisa, or absolutely hated it. It can be so much fun if you let yourself have fun with it. I'd like to think you'd love it. I don't think you'll ever make it to Italy though to see it for yourself so I guess it doesn't really matter. One day, I will look at a pair of blue eyes and not think of you.

— R

Rome, Italy

May 23rd, 2019
Rome, Italy

A place
I never thought I would
return—
I suppose my old coin
in the Trevi fountain
had to fulfill
its purpose eventually.
I look to this city now
to teach me the beauty in chaos—
to find the ancient wisdom
among the present,
the see the genuine within the lies.
This is your second chance.
I'm listening.
Rome, my darling,
seduce me.

May 24th, 2019
Temple of Diana
Rome, Italy

I can sense a warrior spirit
emanating from these marble pillars
like a life force—
this place breathes courage
into the sisters
who have forgotten
how powerful they can be.
Here I pray, to whoever
may be listening,
for the strength to fight
until the sun rises,
for the endurance
to withstand
this war within my chest,
and for the bravery
to allow myself to
feel
again.

ROMA

Fontana di Trevi

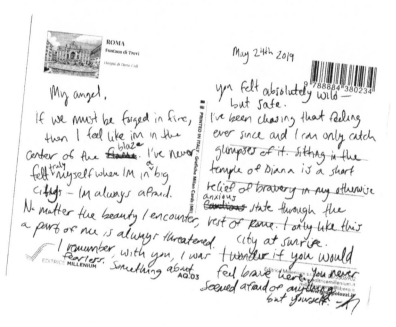

May 24th, 2019 — Rome, Italy

My Angel,

If we must be forged in fire, then I feel like I'm in the center of
the blaze. I've never felt truly myself when I'm in a big city—
I'm always afraid. No matter the beauty I encounter, a part of me
is always threatened. I remember, with you, I was fearless.
Something about you felt absolutely wild— but safe. I've been
chasing that feeling ever since and I can only catch glimpses of it.
Sitting in the temple of Diana is a short relief of bravery in my
otherwise anxious state through the rest of Rome. I only like this
city at sunrise. I wonder if you would feel brave here.
You never seemed afraid of anything but yourself.

—R

TEMPIETTO DI DIANA

Naples, Italy

May 25th, 2019
Train to Naples, Italy

He reminds me of you in the most
obscure ways— the veins in his wrists
look like tangled tree branches.
A memory floods my vision,
the night you held my hands,
kissed the words flowing
from my fingertips,
how I traced the letters of the tattoo
on your forearm. A leaf falls.
I shook my head and dismissed the thought,
letting the memory fall through my hair.

I find myself caught up in
his reflection in the window,
he's chewing on his lip.
You always used to do that while I talked—
driving me crazy. "I'm full of bad habits,"
you'd say. If only I'd listened.
His curious blue eyes crossed mine
and when they looked at me,
they didn't look away—
This made my heart sink into my stomach,
almost the same way as when I first saw you,
it's the kind of look that says
"I want to know you."

I looked away, out to the sea,
never to turn back.
Don't be foolish, silly girl—
close your eyes.
You learned long ago that
you're better off
alone.

May 26th, 2019
Castellammare di Stabia, Italy

It's an uncharacteristically cold morning in
southern Italy where the sun is supposed to
be everlasting. As I sit here with only the
rain endlessly falling to keep me company—
I can see two lovers in the mist
slow dancing high above the city lights.
It's a warm summer evening in their world
lit by starlight and a dying candle flame.
Not a single cloud in the sky as they sweep
across the veranda like two feathers caught
together in the wind. I can see them like the
ghosts of a love I once knew— holding each
other like a memory. I can almost feel their
love reaching out through the fog like a
ray of sunlight fighting to remind me that
warmth is still possible.
Then the rain takes over again and I am
alone.

I pretend the sounds of the storm are string
instruments and dance barefoot through icy
puddles, finding a heartbreaking kind of
joy in this moment distorted between reality
and fantasy. I can almost feel his hand take
mine, then disappearing with the wind— but
if I just close my eyes he's there for sure
and I can hear the music vividly, I can feel
the burn of sunshine, the scent of jasmine,
the taste of wine. Maybe— this moment of
honest longing, daydreaming means I still
have some hope left inside of me.
A kind of hope that I thought was stolen
away long ago. I just have to keep
searching. I just have to find it.

May 27th, 2019
A garden overlooking Naples, Italy

Little red koi fish create
ripples around the lily pads
while the honeybees are hard at work
buzzing from clover to clover—
seagulls soar high above
all I can ever wish to be
and a lone sailboat
skims the horizon—
lost in the sun rays
that have finally found their way
through the fog.

Mount Vesuvius is covered
in all the dark clouds
from the morning storm
and I hope she knows
it won't last
forever.

In this moment
I am only an observer,
but in this lifetime
I want to be
so much more.

May 28th, 2019
Pompeii, Italy

The sun rises in a vision of radiant scarlett
splendor as morning casts its magic
over crumbled houses and the rubble
of lives lost long ago— so long ago,
there's no one left to miss them.
But I do.
I can hear them in the busy streets, the
laughter of young children skipping over
cobblestones, bustling markets, whispers
between a couple holding hands around the
corner, maybe even music.
Walking through this place is like existing
in two different worlds at once.
One is based in a destroyed reality,
the other taking shape
in a thriving imagination.
The walls are faded now, but the
striking crimson covering the frescos
remains, painting the streets, markets, and
homes in the daring color of the very fire
that burned it all away.
There is an unmistakable energy in this
place— a clinging of life in every fallen
pillar, misplaced mosaic,
and wingless statue—
I can feel it in the air that weaves its way
through the ruins and I can see it in every
red poppy that grows among the destruction.

The little red flowers are what caught my
eye more than anything, clustered together
like families holding onto hope.

If every poppy is a soul lost
then they will live on,
despite the dark clouds overhead—
filling this place with life once again.

May 28th, 2019 — Pompeii, Italy

My Angel,

I keep thinking about the poppies in Pompeii. How somewhere
that is known for its tragedy can be filled with so much beauty.
This postcard is of "The house of the tragic poet". I never found it.
I wonder who it belonged to. I suppose in a way every poet is a
tragedy. After all, we were all forged in heartbreak. I wonder
what made you a poet. I don't think I ever asked.
Maybe we can be like the poppies in Pompeii. Tragic— but
beautiful. Maybe that's all we'll ever be. Maybe that's okay.

-R

POMPEI - Cave Canem
Casa del Poeta Tragico
Maison du Poéte Tragique
House of the Tragic Poet
Haus des Trauerspieldichters

© Carcavallo editore - Napoli
Via L. Einaudi, 10 - Tel. 081-204694

RIPRODUZIONE VIETATA

May 28th 2019

My angel,
    I keep thinking about
the poppies in pompeii. How
Somewhere that is known
for it's tragedy can be
filled with so much beauty.
This postcard is of "The
house of the tragic poet". I
never fand it. I wonder who

it belonged to. I suppose
in a way, every poet is a
tragedy. After all, we were
all forged in heartbreak.
I wonder what made you
a poet. I don't think I
ever asked.
Maybe we can be like
the poppies in pompeii.
Tragic- but beautiful.
Maybe that's all we'll ever
be. Maybe that's
okay.

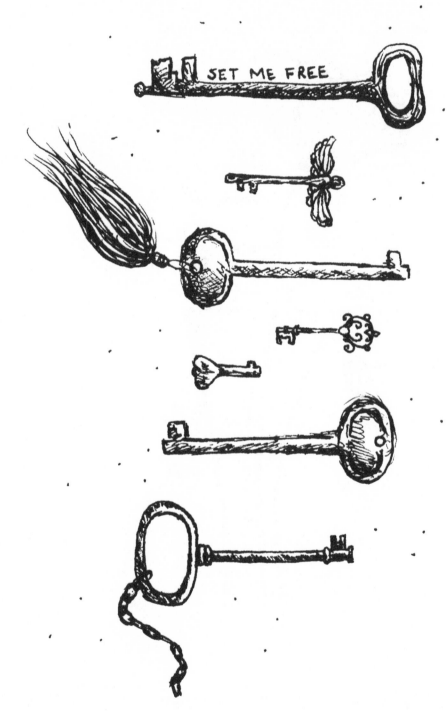

May 29th, 2019
Naples, Italy

She gathers keys
from all over the world
in hopes of finding one
that will finally unlock his heart again—

but no matter how many she collects,
ornate gold, silver of all different sizes,
skeleton brass, not a single one
will open the empty cage
that resides in his chest.

A part of her knows that
he has no love left to give her,
but that will never stop her
from trying another key.

May 30th, 2019
Plane to Thessaloniki, Greece

Two strangers, who may not even be able
to speak the same language,
play the piano together
in a bustling airport—
off to the corner,
filling the whole place with music
for the simple fact
of wanting to hear it.

People are drawn in like
the ocean tide and for a few
minutes we look up at each other,
we stop rushing, we remember
how amazing it feels to smile.

Maybe that's the whole point
to this existence— to humanity.
These little moments of connection.

I will never be in this place again,
I will never see these people again,
but we will all share this memory
of the time when two strangers
turned an airport waiting room
into a concert hall.
When music mattered more
than all our worries combined.

May 30th 2019

NAPOLI · MUSEO NAZIONALE
Pittura · Peinture · Painting · Malerei
Diana cacciatrice (da Stabia)
Diane chasseresse (de Stabia)
Diane the huntress (from Stabia)
Diana als Jägerin (aus Stabia)

My angel,

I was drawn to this post card because I thought she was an angel. She looked sad but brave. It turns out its a fresco of Diana. Artemis. I keep being drawn to her. She never fell in love, as far as I remember. At least, she was alone. She wanted to be.

Maybe its okay to want to be. I dont want love, and that has nothing to do with you anymore. It has to do with me. Just because I dont want love now doesnt mean I wont want it forever. Maybe I'll never change, maybe I will. I cant say. But right now, IM flying 36,000 feet above the clouds and when I think of you there — it doesnt feel like anything.

It doesnt feel like anything.

—R

May 30th, 2019 – Naples, Italy

My Angel,

I was drawn to this postcard because at first I thought she was an angel. She looked sad, & brave. It turns out it's a fresco of Diana. Artemis. I keep being drawn to her. She never fell in love, as far as I remember. At least, she was alone. She wanted to be. Maybe it's okay to want to be. I don't want love, and that has nothing to do with you anymore. It has to do with me. Just because I don't want love now doesn't mean I won't want it forever. Maybe I'll never change. Maybe I will. I can't say. But right now, I'm flying 36,000 feet above the clouds and when I think of you here— it doesn't hurt. It doesn't feel like anything.

—R

May 31st, 2019
Volos, Greece

Sometimes,
I wonder why I ever do
anything else than this
constant travel. This kind of life,
always on the move.

Why do I subject myself to routine,
to settling, to jobs I hate
and getting stuck in them.
Why can't I just pick up
everything— run as fast as I can
and never look back?

Then I remember
birds do have wings for a reason—
for every being needs
some kind of freedom,
but they also have nests
to come back home to

and there is no shame
in needing a nest.

Skopelos, Greece

June 1st, 2019
Skopelos, Greece

It took several glasses of wine
and losing myself in the back streets
of a small island off the coast of Greece
for me to remember that I never needed
you.

I just need to believe it
for longer than thirty seconds.

I don't need anyone—
I can be drunkenly happy
and hopelessly lost all on my own and
the bougainvillea flowers are just as
beautiful as if you
were walking next to me.

God, why did I let this
happen.

I would continue to lie,
but I wish you
here.
Maybe it's just the wine talking,
part of me hopes it is.
Part of me wants
to hold your hand.

June 2nd, 2019
On a sailboat in Greece

That's the thing about
strangers—
it only takes one conversation
to turn them into lifelong friends

and how extraordinary that is,
that bold compassion born in
honesty.
That longing
for empathy. For connection.

Imagine,
if every soul in this world
cared for each other
in the way
I now care for you—
how magnificent
we could be.

June 3rd, 2019
Kastani Beach, Greece

Some places are so beautiful
they hurt—
it's a strange occurrence,
feeling absolutely heartbroken
in a place of such immense beauty.

I'm not entirely sure
why I feel this way.

Maybe it's the thought
that it won't last
forever,
one day it will inevitably be gone—
maybe it's the idea that when I leave
there is a very real possibility
that I will never
see this place again
or maybe
it's the fact that I'm here,
experiencing something
absolutely breathtaking—
and all I can think about is
you.

Skopelos
Agios Joannis

HELLAS GREECE GRECE GRECIA GRIECHENLAND GRECIA

POST CARD   June 3rd 2019

My angel,
Have you ever been Somewhere
so beautiful, it makes you sad?
When I walked the path to
Kastani beach, surrounded by
unbelievable scenery + sunshine—
it broke my heart.
Isn't that strange?
It was a good kind of sad, I think
a necessary pain that
Greetings from Skopelos...

reminds me that nothing
lasts forever and there's
nothing I can do about it.
Not even stars live forever.
I think thats why things that
are so temporary — humans,
flowers, stars, love — are so
beautiful, they hurt. Because
you know one day, they will
die. -R

Zahos Stamoulis PHOTOGRAPHY ★ @: zahostamoulis@gmail.com ★ www.zahosartphoto.gr ★ Tel.+30 6972841329 SKOPELOS   A101

June 3rd, 2019 — Skopelos, Greece

My Angel,

Have you ever been somewhere so beautiful, it makes you sad?
When I walked the path to Kastani beach, surrounded by
unbelievable scenery & sunshine— it broke my heart. Isn't that
strange? It was a good kind of sad I think, a necessary pain that
reminded me that nothing lasts forever and there's nothing I can
do about it. Not even stars live forever. I suppose that's why things
that are so temporary— humans, flowers, stars, love— are so
beautiful, they hurt. Because you know one day, they will die.

-R

June 4th, 2019
Skopelos Port, Greece

And when he kissed me I didn't feel
fireworks, I don't know what I was expecting
but I didn't feel sparks, I didn't feel
anything.

That's the thing about losing touch
with your heart altogether—
you practically cease to exist.

When he touched me I felt
the ghost of your lips and nothing more.
Nothing has felt brand new since you.
I thought maybe
if I try again— another kiss—
still nothing.
As his hands explored my body I realized
I couldn't feel
anything at all.

No matter how many strangers I take
a chance on, it never changes.
I try and try and try
to make myself feel, but I always end up
even more empty than before.

I don't know
what happened to me, I don't know
what took it all away—
how I ended up left out in the cold.
I would love to blame you
but something tells me
that the only person I can blame is
myself.

June 5th, 2019
Agios Ioannis Kastri
Skopelos, Greece

It seems so pointless—
searching for something
that I wouldn't even be able to handle
if I find it. I woke up today,
numb to believing in something more,
to everything I used to dream of.

My heart doesn't skip a beat anymore,
it hardly beats at all.

I don't know what else to do.

As I sit here and
write these words
I see a dandelion growing
just an arm's-length away.
I've always been a believer
in wishmaking,
so here goes nothing—

I pluck the little weed,
blow away its feather seeds,
and wish
for a love I can
feel.

DOORS OF GREECE

June 5th, 2019 – Skopelos, Greece

My Angel,

It's late here and the past few nights the stars have been brighter
because of the new moon. I have to be honest— I feel lost. Maybe it's
because the moon isn't here to guide me. I feel like I'm drifting.
Last night, I kissed a stranger— I felt nothing. I don't feel much of
anything anymore— at least not in the sense of love. I haven't felt
much of anything since you.

-R

June 5th 2019

POST CARD

My angel,
   its late here and
the past few nights the
stars have been brighter
because of the new moon.
I have to be honest —
I feel a bit lost. Maybe
its because the Moon
isnt here to listen
or guide me.

I feel like Im drifting.
Last night, I kissed a
stranger – I felt nothing.
I dont feel much of
anything anymore –
at least not in the
sense of love: I havent
felt much of anything
since you. -R

ploos
DESIGN

Designed & made in Greece

June 6th, 2019
Skopelos Lookout, Greece

I suppose it was a lesson
I had to learn, I will never be able
to reach everyone
at the depth I would like to—
some people are just too afraid
of deep water.

I want to believe
everyone I take a chance on
is meant to be significant, but
sometimes they are only ever meant
to disappoint.

Sometimes he's only ever meant
to wear feather soft sheepskin
and honey sweet kisses
until the moment comes when
he turns vile.
It was once he realized
I wouldn't give him what he wanted.

When I stood my ground
it was as if instantaneously—
every speck of human compassion
was thrown out the window,
as if I never mattered
in the first place.

Treated like sand to be swept away
by the ocean and forgotten.
Yet here I am
still wondering what I did wrong.

ARTEMIS

June 7th, 2019 – Skopelos, Greece

My Angel,

I'm leaving Greece today and I feel like I've learned so much, but I still have so far to go. I met an older woman that reminded me of the moon and she told me that maybe I don't feel anything because I'm in a period of grieving. Because I'm protecting myself. That I'm not afraid or against falling in love— I'm afraid and against losing it. I know what that feels like and I know how much it hurts and why would anyone want to go through that again? She said it was okay. I told her about you. She said it sounds like I'm writing to a version of you that I wish you could be. That I wish we could have been. Maybe so. She said she believes in me, and that might just be enough for me to start believing in myself.

                                                              —R

London, England

June 7th, 2019
Plane to London, England

The entire sky is alive with light
and that has to mean something—
we've been flying
into the same horizon for hours now,
caught in the sunset,
and I've never had to look him in the eyes
for so long. I've been avoiding the sun
for a while now, and yet I always seem to
find myself engulfed by him.
I never wanted to face him
again, I am still angry with him
for leaving me over and over.

Why couldn't you have just stayed?
It's too cold in this sky without you.
What is the moon
without her sun? Tell me—
what am I to do without you?

Silence. Always silence.

Forget it, I'll go.
Let me go.

Let me let you go.

Just let me cloak myself
in shadow.

June 8th, 2019
Gatsby's Drugstore
London, England

There's something
about a bouquet
of cut flowers
on the table
that is so tragically
beautiful. I wonder
where they came from—
if they were ever wild,
if they were ever free.
Did they put up a fight
or go willingly?

What kind of person
loves a wildflower enough
to let it grow
and what kind of person
rips it from its home?

A single daisy catches my eye,
withering away from the others—
petals falling one by one,
which begs the question:
He loves me? He loves me not?

He loves me.
He loves me not.

June 9th, 2019
Hyde Park
London, England

I wish more people
could look at the world
and see the wonder in it before the
destruction.
To search for the shining souls
of every living thing
and pronounce them magnificent
instead of denying them value
for the sake of convenience.
I wish more people
could hold out their hands
and actually want
you to take them. I wish
more people could invite truth
into their voices
and forgiveness into their hearts
and I think
what I'm trying to say is—
I wish more people could be
a little more like you.

June 10th, 2019
Natural History Museum
London, England

At this point I don't know
if the moon is following me,
or if I'm following her.
She always shows herself
when I need her the most—
like a beacon guiding me
through the darkness.

I'd like to think
I could be a beacon
for her as well—
maybe I don't shine as bright
and maybe I don't have the strength
to push and pull the tides,
but I can be there to listen
and do my best to understand
and maybe that can be
enough.

June 10th, 2019 – London, England

My Angel,

Something magic happened tonight— two people from literally the other side of the world went out of their way to find their way to me, to show me a kind of love I didn't know I needed.

Poetry brought them to me, and in a way— you brought them to me. All of them. Maybe it isn't the love I've always "wanted" but it is the love I need. I have all the love I need. While he held my hand and she rested her head on my shoulder— time stopped. I felt love— a new kind. Maybe I'm not meant for the old kind— I'm meant to move forward.

Thank you. Please forgive me. I'm sorry. I love you.

-R

My angel ~~~~~~~~~~~~~~~~~~~~~ June 10th 2019

Something magic happened tonight— two people from literally the other side of the world went out of their way to find their way to me, to show me a kind of love I didn't know I needed. Poetry brought them to me, and in a way— you brought them to me. All of them. Maybe it isn't the love I've always "wanted" but it is the love I need. I have all the love I need. While he held my hand and she rested her head on my shoulder— time stopped. I felt love— a new kind. Maybe I'm not meant for the old kind—I'm meant to move forward. Thank you. Please forgive me. I'm sorry. I love you. -R

June 11th, 2019
Plane to New York City

I hate to say that I miss you,
but I think you know I do.
I'm quite sure
a part of me always will—
no matter how far I drift,
how much time passes,
or who's arms I fall into.
I started this journey believing
that made me utterly pathetic, weak,
hopeless—
but none of that is true.
It never was. I know now—
the everlasting ceaseless inevitable
missing of you
means I felt something real—
and that is proof enough
that one day I can feel it again.

My angel,

I couldn't find a postcard so this boarding pass will do. This plane, taking me home, is about to take off and I keep thinking of all the goodbyes I've said recently. To beautiful places, to incredible strangers turned lifelong friends. Their goodbye wasn't easy but there was a sweetness in knowing I will see them again. I think I've put off telling you goodbye because I know there will never be another goodbye — at least not to the man I fell in love with. I have to say goodbye to him well. It doesn't hurt as much as I thought it would. I'm not completely stitched for good. I think that okay. I've always loved finding up but I don't think I ever will be. I think that's okay. I've always loved finding the beauty in broken things anyway. This will be the last time I write to you. It's time to let you go, to fly away. It's time to look →

---

norwegian

BOARDING PASS:

BOARDING TIME:	GATE:	SEAT:	BOARDING GROUP:
15:45		**32D**	**PRIO**

FLIGHT NO: D1 7015   DATE: 11JUN

NAME: CLIFT/RACHEL MS
FROM: LONDON/LGW
TO: NEW YORK/JFK

DEPARTURE TIME:	BOARDING GROUP:
17:05	PRIO
CLASS:	SEAT:
Y	32D

CLIFT/RACHEL MS
DI 7015 11JUN
FROM: LONDON/LGW
TO: NEW YORK/JFK

forward to my own bright horizon instead of up to the PRIO Clouds. We're taking off now. By thistime we land you will be gone — immortalized in nothing but ink. This is my path now — to walk without you. Goodbye, my love, just please —

SEQUENCE 070 [...]
my love
well. XX

June 17th, 2019 – London, England

My Angel,

I couldn't find a postcard so this boarding pass will do. This plane taking me home is about to take off and I keep thinking of all the goodbyes I've said recently. Time and time again. To beautiful places, to incredible strangers turned lifelong friends. Their goodbyes weren't easy, but there was a sweetness in knowing I will see them again. I think I've put off telling you goodbye because I know there will never be another hello — at least not to the man I fell in love with. I have to say goodbye to him for good. It doesn't hurt as much as I thought it would. I'm not completely stitched up, but I don't think I ever will be. I think that's okay.

I've always loved finding the beauty in the broken things anyway. This will be the last time I write to you. It's time to let you fly away. It's time to look forward to my own bright horizon instead of up to the clouds — We're taking off now. By the time we land you will be gone — immortalized in nothing but ink. This is my path now — to walk without you. Just please don't go to Budapest.

Goodbye, my love.
I hope you remember me well.

xx – R

June 12th, 2019
Plane to Knoxville, Tennessee

Some things may become easier with practice,
but saying goodbye will never be one of them.

This goodbye tastes bittersweet
when spilling from my lips,
because I know there will be
a hello again.

It's only a matter of when,
as so many of my heartstrings are tied
to little islands in Greece,
winding streets of Italy,
sailboats in Spain,
and found again soulmates—
to all of these I am tethered,
and happy to be so.

One day, one day soon,
we will be together once more—
and oh, how I am looking forward
to that sun rising.

To all that I have loved,
until we meet again.

Thank you for reliving this journey with me,
for holding this hope in your hands,
for treating these words with grace, allowing
them to be not only just memory, but a reverie
to soothe the ache of those who still need to say
goodbye.

To all my runaway broken hearts—
I hear you,
I understand you, I need you to know
you are not alone in this.

xx Rachel

Made in the USA
Coppell, TX
27 November 2020

42247141R00069